Wisteria

Place

A House of History and Haunting

Patricia Shannon Evans

TIBBEE TALES
PUBLISHING

Published by Tibbee Tales
Columbus, MS 39705
Copyright 2025 by Patricia Shannon Evans
All rights reserved
All illustrations are from the author's collection and the collection of the Billups-Garth Archives at the Columbus-Lowndes Public Library unless otherwise noted.
First published in 2025
Manufactured in the United States
979-8-9931019-0-3
Evans, Patricia Shannon
Wisteria Place: A House of History and Haunting/Patricia Shannon Evans. p.cm.
Includes bibliographical references.
979-8-9931019-0-3

1. Mississippi History–William Cannon (MS and AL) --History 2. Alabama History–Alexander Meek (AL and MS) 3. Antebellum South–Columbus, MS (MS and AL) 4. Alexander Meek–Balaklava Poem (AL) 5. Alexander Meek–Attorney General (AL) 6. Ghost Story–Civil War Era Apparition (MS)

Awaiting Library of Congress Number

Historical Silences in Research

In the process of researching and documenting the history of Columbus, Mississippi, I am acutely aware of the profound limitations in my ability to fully represent the lived experiences of enslaved individuals. The historical record has systematically marginalized and erased the voices, stories, and individual identities of those who were enslaved, creating significant challenges for comprehensive historical scholarship. The scarcity of primary source materials directly related to enslaved populations presents a critical research obstacle. Archival records often:

- Reduce individuals to property inventories
- Omit personal narratives
- Minimize human complexity
- Perpetuate systemic historical erasure

While acknowledging the limitations of this current research, I remain committed to recognizing the humanity of enslaved individuals. I hope myself and other historians learn to present available historical information with respect and nuance and create space for more comprehensive future scholarship.

This acknowledgement is not an endpoint, but a critical starting point for more comprehensive historical understanding.

Patricia Shannon Evans, Author

Acknowledgements

I would like to express my deepest gratitude to my "family" for their unwavering support throughout this journey. To Himself, who endured late nights and countless revisions with a smile, and to my fellow childhood friend and editor Kate Doster Wright, who inspired me with her boundless imagination.

A special thanks to my cousin Billy Cox, for believing in this project and championing it tirelessly. The entire archive team at the Lowndes County Library (especially Mona Vance-Ali) deserves applause for their insightful feedback, support, and dedication to shaping this project.

Heartfelt thanks to my writing accountability pal, author Julie Liddell Whitehead, whose constructive criticism and constant encouragement kicked my backside when needed. I also would like to thank my dear sweet friend Rachel Baskerville George who keeps me on track and keeps me digging into Columbus history to answer all manner of questions.

This book would not be the same without the exceptional cover design by Paxton Garrard. His creativity brought the story to life. My marketing lead in all of this is Andrew "AJ" Woody. His insights and hard work are greatly appreciated. I love my team and all they have done to support me on this project and how they pushed me over the finish line.

Finally, to the readers who love history, thank you for giving these homes and our beautiful town a place in your heart.

Never Would I Have Believed...

Little did I know when I bought Wisteria Place that it was built by an ancestor, William Cannon. Maybe I should clarify: This house was built *for* an ancestor…not by an ancestor. It was designed by a local famous architect and built by enslaved people. Someone stated, "to visit Columbus without visiting Wisteria Place is like going to the Nation's capital and not going to see The White House."

That's one thing about owning a home steeped in rich history and still revealing its stories. Its bones are over 170 years old, and it is still being lived in just like any other home. Two barking beagles racing up and down the stairs, lots of entertainment parties, visits from friends who are curious about the place. This house still rings of life and will continue do so for the next 170 years.

To me, an antebellum home is only as historic as the people who lived here. Poor Mr. Cannon died just a year after the house was completed. His widow wasted no time and married a prominent politician, Mr. Alexander B. Meek.

Back then rich people married rich people. That is the situation Mrs. Cannon faced when her husband died. She needed to follow the money, which is exactly what she did. I've been told that my ancestry is a wreath instead of a family tree because it seems I'm related in some way to all the old families of Columbus, Mississippi and Lowndes County.

From stories I've heard that may or may not be true, like the duel supposedly fought in the side yard of Wisteria Place. And the clip-clop of a horse carrying a Confederate soldier led by an enslaved man up the street and into the back of the place. To the sudden aroma of cigar smoke or perfume when no one is around. I don't question these things, because to believe in such is to experience such. And then there are the stories that *are* true such as the visit by future Confederate President Jefferson Davis to see his best friend Mr. Cannon at a supper party at Wisteria Place.

Personalities are also a large part of the story of Wisteria Place. General Brownrigg, a significant planter in the area who built Temple Heights for his town home as a replica of a Greek temple on a city block. He sold ½ of the land to the Cannons to build their home behind his. Across the street is the Dowsing-Banks-Foote home, where my grandfather was born. Everywhere you look in Columbus there are connections to history and often one's own past.

All these people were friends, enemies, contentious at times and on good terms most of the time. For Columbus to thrive, these early pioneers had to work together, where it be as planters, politicians, school administrators, poets, champion chess players, or just plain common folk. They all lived among each other, with each other, and despite each other. I am proud the residents of Wisteria Place played a role in that. Thank you for allowing me to share its history with you.

Billy Cox and John Carr
Current owners of Wisteria Place

The Birth of a Grand Antebellum Home

In the heart of Columbus, Mississippi, stands a magnificent antebellum mansion known as Wisteria Place. This stately home, with its rich history and whispered tales of ghostly encounters, offers a fascinating glimpse into the lives of wealthy Southern planters in the mid-19th century. The house, with its grand columns and expansive porches, is a prime example of Greek Revival architecture popular in the American South during this period.

Our story begins with William Cannon, a prosperous Prairie planter who sought to provide his children with better educational opportunities. After a devastating fire consumed his Mayhew Plantation Home on the prairie in 1852, Cannon established a town residence in Columbus. He purchased a half-city block lot from the Harris family, who owned the nearby Temple Heights property at the time. This move was typical of wealthy planters of the era, who often maintained rural plantations and urban residences to balance their agricultural interests with social and educational pursuits.

To bring his vision to life, Cannon enlisted the services of James Lull, a talented architect from Vermont. Lull's Northern background brought  a unique perspective to Southern architecture, blending elements of New England design with the grandeur expected of a Southern mansion. Construction of Wisteria Place began in 1852 and was completed by 1854.

The house stood as a testament to Cannon's wealth and refined taste, boasting an impressive collection of family portraits, Austrian China, English silver, and imported Bohemian glass. The interior featured high ceilings, ornate plasterwork, and grand fireplaces in every room. The parlor showcased luxury with its crystal chandeliers and imported French wallpaper.

Sadly, William Cannon's time in his new home was short-lived. He passed away in 1858, just four years after the house was completed. However, some say that Cannon's spirit never left Wisteria Place. Visitors and residents alike have reported sightings of a ghostly figure in the side yard, dressed in shirt sleeves and a waistcoat, appearing hurried or forgetful.

One particularly vivid account comes from a groundskeeper in the 1920s, who described seeing a translucent figure pacing near the old servants' quarters, muttering about cotton prices and crop yields. This spectral presence is believed to be William Cannon himself, forever tied to the home he so lovingly created and the business concerns that occupied his mind and life.

The Cannon-Meek Home - A Window into Antebellum Columbus

Facing 8th Street North in Columbus, Mississippi, stands a stately home that has witnessed over 165 years of history. Known today as Wisteria Place, this grand residence was originally built in 1854 by Colonel William R. Cannon and later was known as the Meek Home.

The house earned its name from the Meek family, who occupied it for several generations. Colonel Cannon's daughter, Sarah Elizabeth Cannon, married Samuel M. Meek in 1855, establishing the family's connection to the property. After William Cannon's death, his widow married Alexander B. Meek, a well-known poet and lawyer of the time. This union further cemented the Meek name in the annals of the home's history.

Alexander B. Meek was not only a poet but also served as the Attorney General of Alabama and authored several historical works. His most famous poem, "The

Red Eagle," told the story of William Weatherford, a Creek Indian chief. Meek's literary pursuits and political connections helped elevate the home's status as a cultural center in Columbus.

The Meek Home quickly became a hub for social and political gatherings in Columbus. Its guest list reads like a who's who of 19th-century Mississippi:

-*Jefferson Davis,* future President of the Confederacy, attended a banquet here in 1860 during a political campaign. Davis, then a U.S. Senator, was touring Mississippi to rally support for the Southern cause. His visit to the Meek Home underscored its importance as a political meeting place.

- *Governors John A. Quitman*, William McWillie and John J. McRae were all guests at various times. Governor Quitman, who served as governor from 1835 to 1836 and again from 1850 to 1851, was known for his strong pro-slavery stance and his support for the annexation of Texas.

- *General Nathan Bedford Forrest*, the controversial Confederate cavalry leader and later president of the Selma, Marion, and Memphis Railroad, was a frequent house guest of Colonel Meek. Forrest's visits likely occurred after the Civil War, during his time as a railroad executive, reflecting the home's continued importance in the post-war era.

The home's reputation for hospitality was so renowned that in 1883, following a meeting of the Mississippi Press Association, the Yazoo Herald declared: "To visit Columbus and not visit Colonel Meek's home would be like leaving out the Capitol when going to Washington."

This comparison to the nation's capital highlights the Meek Home's significance in Mississippi's social and political landscape. The home likely hosted numerous dinner parties, political discussions, and cultural events that shaped the state's trajectory during the tumultuous years before and after the Civil War.

The Meek Home is a prime example of old colonial architecture, reflecting the Greek Revival style popular in the antebellum South. The multi-colored Venetian glass surrounding the doorway has a luxurious touch that speaks to the wealth and taste of its original owners. The wide central hallway, typical of homes in the Deep South, was designed to improve air circulation in the hot, humid climate. It has a symmetrical façade with evenly spaced windows and a central entrance, hallmarks of the Greek Revival style.

Now known as Wisteria Place, the home stands at the corner of 6th Avenue North and 8th Street North, just behind another historic Columbus landmark, Temple Heights. The name likely comes from the large wisteria vine locked in a century-long battle with an equally impressive magnolia tree in the front yard.

This intertwining of wisteria and magnolia serves as a living metaphor for the home's history - the delicate, climbing wisteria represents the social connections and cultural refinement of the home's past, the sturdy, evergreen magnolia symbolizes the enduring strength and Southern roots of the property.

While Wisteria Place is not currently listed on the National Register of Historic Places, it remains an important part of Columbus's architectural heritage. As of 2023, it has been included in the city's annual Pilgrimage tour after an eight-year hiatus, and it continues to be a point of interest for history enthusiasts.

Efforts to preserve the home and its contents are ongoing. Local historical societies and preservationists work to maintain the structure and educate the public about its significance. These efforts include regular maintenance of the building's exterior to protect it from weather damage and careful cataloging and preservation of the home's historical artifacts. Research continues into the home's history and its connections to important figures in Mississippi's past.

From its role in antebellum social life to its preservation of 19th-century artifacts, this home offers a unique glimpse into the past. As we conclude our tour of this historic residence, we're reminded of the importance of preserving such landmarks for future generations to learn from and enjoy.

The story of the Cannon-Meek Home is not just about a building or a single family. It's a window into the complex social, political, and cultural landscape of the 19th-century South. Through its walls, we can better understand the interconnected lives of politicians, soldiers, poets, and everyday citizens who shaped Mississippi's history. As we face forward into the future, homes like Wisteria Place serve as crucial links to our past, helping us to understand where we've come from and informing the path ahead.

Economic Turmoil and the Missouri Compromise

The early 19th century brought significant challenges to the young United States. In 1819, a financial panic swept across the country, marking the beginning of America's first peacetime economic crisis. This downturn affected all aspects of American life and lasted until 1821. Trade growth came to an abrupt halt, with exports falling by 25% between 1818 and 1819. Unemployment rates soared, reaching as high as 75% in some urban areas. Banks failed, with over 40% of banks closing their doors by 1821. Mortgages were foreclosed, leading to widespread homelessness. Agricultural prices fell by half, devastating farmers across the country. Investment in western lands collapsed, halting westward expansion.

Several interconnected factors contributed to this economic disaster:

> 1. A dramatic decline in cotton prices: Cotton fell from 32 cents per pound in 1818 to 14 cents in

1819, primarily due to overproduction and increased competition from India and Egypt.

2. The Bank of the United States' credit contraction: To curb inflation, the Second Bank of the United States raised interest rates and called in loans, leading to a severe credit crunch.

3. An 1817 congressional order requiring hard-currency payments for land purchases: This policy shift made it more difficult for speculators and settlers to buy western lands, cooling the land boom.

4. Closure of many factories due to foreign competition: The end of the War of 1812 led to an influx of cheap British goods, forcing many American manufacturers out of business.

5. Overexpansion of credit: Banks had issued too many loans and paper money, leading to inflation and economic instability.

As the nation grappled with economic turmoil, a new crisis emerged that would shake the foundations of the Union. The application of Missouri for statehood in 1819 ignited a fierce debate over the status of slavery west of the Mississippi River. Thomas Jefferson described this sudden eruption as a "fireball in the night," recognizing its potential to tear the nation apart.

After intense negotiations and debate lasting nearly two years, a compromise was finally reached. Missouri was admitted as a slave state, maintaining the delicate balance between free and slave states in the Senate. Maine, previously part of Massachusetts, was admitted as a free state to preserve the sectional balance. Slavery was prohibited in the Louisiana Purchase territory north of the 36° 30' north latitude line, except within the borders of Missouri itself.

Henry Clay, known as the "Great Compromiser," played a crucial role in steering this compromise through Congress. He convinced a handful of antislavery representatives to support the proposal in the interest of preserving the Union, arguing that compromise was essential to prevent a potential civil war.

While the Missouri Compromise temporarily resolved the crisis, it was clear that the underlying sectional conflict remained unresolved. Both Jefferson and John Quincy Adams recognized that this was merely a postponement of a larger, looming conflict.

The South faced two options to defend its political power against a growing antislavery majority. Forge new political alliances with the North and West. This strategy would involve finding common ground on economic issues, such as tariffs and internal improvements. Or acquire new territory in the Southwest. This option would likely reignite northern opposition and potentially upset the delicate balance established by the Missouri Compromise.

The Missouri Crisis also had significant implications for the existing political party system. The Federalist Party, already in decline, was effectively destroyed by its opposition to the Compromise. The Democratic-Republican Party began to fracture along sectional lines, setting the stage for the emergence of new political parties in the coming decades.

The Panic of 1819 and the Missouri Crisis revealed deep-seated economic and political tensions within the

The Missouri Compromise
1820

young nation. While compromise had been achieved, the geographical line drawn by the Missouri Compromise would continue to be a source of conflict. As Jefferson prophetically wrote, this line, "once conceived and held up to the angry passions of men, will never be obliterated; and every new irritation will mark it deeper and deeper."

The events of this period set the stage for future conflicts and debates that would ultimately lead to the Civil War, shaping the course of American history for decades to come. Some of the long-term consequences included increased sectionalism. The compromise highlighted the growing divide between North and South. The rise of abolitionism created public debate over slavery during the Missouri Crisis and helped fuel the abolitionist movement. The Panic of 1819 led to calls for greater government intervention in the economy and sparked debates over the role of banks and currency. The compromise set a precedent for how new states would be admitted to the Union, influencing future territorial acquisitions and statehood debates.

These events of the early 19th century laid the groundwork for the major conflicts and transformations that would define American history in the decades to come and shaped Columbus and the people who settled there.

James Lull - Columbus' Eclectic Architect

In the mid-19th century, a talented architect named James Lull left an indelible mark on the city of Columbus, Mississippi. His unique architectural style, blending Greek Revival with Gothic and Italianate elements, came to be known as "Columbus Eclectic." This chapter explores Lull's life, his significant contributions to Columbus' architectural landscape, and the lasting impact of his work on the city's visual identity and cultural heritage.

James Lull was born in 1814 in Windsor, Vermont, a small town known for its picturesque New England architecture. This early exposure to traditional building styles would later influence his work. He received his education in Philadelphia, Pennsylvania, a city at the forefront of American architecture in the early 19th century. Here, Lull likely encountered the works of renowned architects such as William Strickland and

Thomas U. Walter, whose Greek Revival designs were gaining popularity.

By 1839, at the age of 25, Lull had made his way to Columbus, Mississippi. While the exact reasons for his move remain unclear, it's possible he was drawn by the economic opportunities in the rapidly growing Southern states. Columbus, founded just 20 years earlier, was experiencing a boom period and would have been an attractive destination for a young, ambitious architect.

In 1842, Lull married Francis Tucker in Noxubee County, Mississippi. Francis was the daughter of Pleasant Tucker, a prominent cotton farmer and plantation owner who had received land grants for his service in the Florida Indian Wars. This marriage likely provided Lull with important social connections in the region, which may have helped him secure commissions for his architectural work.

Lull is credited with introducing the Greek Revival style to Columbus, adapting it to suit the Southern climate and lifestyle. His work often featured elements such as imposing columns and porticos, symmetrical facades, low-pitched roofs, elaborate entablatures, and decorative friezes.

Some of Lull's other notable works include:

> *First Baptist Church* (1839) - Originally featuring massive columns, this church demonstrated

Lull's ability to adapt Greek Revival principles to ecclesiastical architecture. The building has since undergone renovations, but elements of Lull's original design remain.

Lowndes County Courthouse (1847) - This iconic building features a prominent clock tower and exemplifies Lull's ability to blend Greek Revival elements with other architectural styles. The courthouse's design includes a symmetrical facade, large columns, and a triangular pediment, all hallmarks of Greek Revival architecture.

Riverview (started c. 1844) - Built for Colonel Charles McLaren, this mansion is considered one of Lull's masterpieces. It features a grand double portico with Ionic columns, expansive windows, and intricate interior details such as carved woodwork and plaster moldings.

Camelia Place (c. 1847) - Lull's own home, a smaller version of Riverview, showcased his personal architectural preferences. The house featured a unique blend of Greek Revival and Italianate styles, with a symmetrical facade, a low-pitched roof, and elaborate cornices.

S.D. Lee Home (1847) - This home incorporates Roman Revival elements, showcasing Lull's versatility as an architect. The house features a distinctive octagonal cupola, which was an unusual element in Southern architecture of the time.

Beyond his architectural work, Lull made significant contributions to Columbus in various ways. He served as a member of the Columbus Selectmen, participating in local governance and urban planning decisions. He acted as a trustee at Franklin Academy, demonstrating his commitment to education in the community. He worked as a weather observer for the Smithsonian Institution for over 15 years, collecting valuable meteorological data that contributed to our understanding of Southern climate patterns.

Callaway Hall – Mississippi University for Women

He designed bridges and an above-ground cistern for Columbus, addressing the city's infrastructure needs.

His bridge designs incorporated innovative engineering techniques of the time, such as truss systems for increased strength and stability. He created an elaborate pumping system to drain area swamps, aiming to reduce the spread of infectious diseases and create more buildable land. This project showcased Lull's understanding of public health issues and his ability to apply engineering solutions to environmental problems.

Lull's unique architectural style, known as Columbus Eclectic, is characterized by a blend of Greek Revival, Gothic, and Italianate elements. This distinctive approach to design set his work apart and left a lasting impression on the city's architectural landscape. Key features of the Columbus Eclectic style include Greek Revival elements including columns, symmetrical facades, and low-pitched roofs. Gothic influences like pointed arches, decorative tracery, and steep gables. And Italianate features with elaborate cornices, wide overhanging eaves, and ornate brackets.

His ability to harmoniously combine these diverse elements resulted in buildings that were both aesthetically pleasing and functionally adapted to the Southern climate. For example, the wide porches and high ceilings common in his designs helped keep interiors cool during hot Mississippi summers.

Lull continued working until his death in 1871. In his will, he left his house and half of his estate to his wife

Florence, with the remainder divided equally among his siblings. This distribution of his assets provides insight into Lull's values and his commitment to both his immediate family and his extended relatives.

Today, many of Lull's designs still stand in Columbus, serving as a testament to his architectural brilliance and enduring impact on the city. His buildings have become integral to Columbus' identity and are frequently featured in historical tours and architectural studies. The preservation of these structures not only honors Lull's legacy but also contributes to the city's cultural tourism industry.

His contributions to Columbus, Mississippi, extend far beyond the buildings he designed. His innovative approach to architecture, civic engagement, and efforts to improve public health have left a legacy. The Columbus Eclectic style he developed continues to be admired and studied, making James Lull a significant figure in the architectural history of the American South.

As a builder, his work represents a unique moment in American architectural history, bridging the gap between the formal classicism of the early 19th century and the more eclectic styles that would emerge in the latter half of the century. His ability to adapt and blend different architectural traditions foreshadowed the creative eclecticism of the Victorian era.

Lull's multifaceted career - as an architect, civic leader, and amateur scientist - exemplifies the ideal of the Renaissance man in 19th-century America. His diverse interests and contributions to Columbus make him not just an important figure in architectural history, but a key player in the broader cultural and social development of the antebellum South.

His work gives valuable insights into the architectural, social, and cultural dynamics of 19th-century Mississippi. Lull's legacy serves as a reminder of the profound impact that one talented and dedicated individual can have on the physical and cultural landscape of a community.

William Rashae Cannon, Sr

In the early 19th century, as economic hardships swept
across the American South, many families sought new
opportunities in the expanding frontier. Among these
pioneers was William Rashae Cannon Sr., born on April
9, 1804, in Darlington, South Carolina. The son of
wealthy landowners Horatio Rashae Cannon and
Elizabeth, he was educated in Columbia, SC where he
would stand out academically and earn his Law degree
there. William would eventually become a prominent
figure in Mississippi's political and social landscape.

The 1830s brought significant challenges to the
Southern states. Exhausted soil, falling crop prices, and
the economic panic of 1837 pushed many families to
seek greener pastures. For instance, cotton prices
plummeted from 17.5 cents per pound in 1831 to just 7.5
cents by 1839, devastating many plantation owners. The
Cannon family, like many others, saw promise in the
newly opened Mississippi Territory. The Treaty of
Dancing Rabbit Creek in 1830 and the displacement of
the Native American inhabitants to Oklahoma, made

vast tracts of land available for settlement, William and his father Rashae set out for Mississippi and a new beginning.

The journey from South Carolina to Mississippi was arduous and fraught with danger. Families like the Cannons often traveled in wagon trains, facing treacherous river crossings, unpredictable weather, and the constant threat of illness. They had to navigate through dense forests and across rugged terrain, often covering only 10-15 miles per day. The trip could take anywhere from several weeks to a few months, depending on the route and conditions.

In 1835, the Cannons arrived in Mississippi, settling near Tibbee Station, a small community in Clay County. Here, they established a large plantation, laying the groundwork for their future success. The Cannons grew cotton, the dominant crop of the region, as well as other staples like corn and tobacco. However, personal tragedy struck when William's first wife passed away, prompting him to return briefly to his home state South Carolina.

William's return to South Carolina proved fortuitous, as he married his cousin, Eliza Jane Cannon. Eliza, a graduate of the Episcopal College in South Carolina, would become an important partner in William's life and endeavors. Her education was unusual for women of the time, reflecting the Cannon family's progressive views on learning. Together, they raised four children: Mary Louisa, Thomas, Susan Ann, and William Jr.

Life on the Cannon plantation was a mix of hard work and Southern gentility. The family likely lived in a large, white-columned house typical of wealthy plantation owners. Their days were filled with overseeing farm operations, managing household affairs, and participating in social events with neighboring families. The children received their early education from private tutors at home before being sent to more formal schools.

William R. Cannon's influence extended beyond his plantation. In 1848, he was elected to the Mississippi Senate as a Democrat, representing Oktibbeha and Chickasaw Counties. His leadership qualities and integrity quickly became apparent, leading to his appointment as President of the Senate, a position he held until 1850. He was good friends with Jefferson Davis who visited the Cannon home whenever he was in Columbus.

During his tenure, Cannon was involved in several important legislative debates. For example, he played a role in discussions about the expansion of the state's railroad system, which was crucial for economic development. He also participated in debates about education funding and the establishment of more public schools in Mississippi.

The Cannons were active members of St. Paul's Church in Columbus, demonstrating their commitment to their new community. William served on the church's vestry and was known for his generous donations to various charitable causes. His involvement in both political and social spheres helped shape the developing state of Mississippi.

In 1854, William completed construction on Wisteria Place, his town home in Columbus. This Greek Revival-style home, with its distinctive columns and spacious rooms, reflected the family's wealth and status. The move was strategic, allowing his children to attend Franklin Academy, the state's first free school. The Cannon family's commitment to education reflected their values and desire to contribute to their adopted state's development.

Wisteria Place quickly became a center of social and cultural life in Columbus. The Cannons hosted elaborate dinner parties and social gatherings, bringing together politicians, businessmen, and other prominent members of society. The home's gardens, featuring the namesake wisteria vines, were particularly admired and became a local attraction.

William R. Cannon Sr.'s time in his new home was brief. He fell gravely ill in 1858, possibly due to a yellow fever outbreak that was common in the region at the time. Despite the best efforts of local doctors, Cannon passed away on April 15th of that year, just four years after moving into Wisteria Place and at the relatively young age of 54.

News of Cannon's death reverberated throughout Mississippi. The state senate adjourned for a day in his honor, and newspapers across the state published lengthy obituaries. He was remembered not just for his political accomplishments, but for his character, described as a model of "purity of life, unbending probity, and kindness of heart." His loss was felt as both a public and private bereavement, a  testament to the impact he had made in his adopted home. Jefferson Davis, U.S. Secretary of War at the time, said, "I have lost my best friend."

After William's death, Eliza Jane continued to manage the family's affairs and raise their children. The Cannon name remained prominent in Mississippi society, with their descendants going on to become successful businessmen, politicians, and community leaders.

William Rashae Cannon Sr.'s life journey from South Carolina to Mississippi mirrors the experiences of many Southern families in the early 19th century. His story is one of adaptation, perseverance, and leadership. Through his political service, community involvement, and personal conduct, Cannon left an indelible mark on Mississippi's history.

His legacy serves as a reminder of the impact one individual can have in shaping a developing state and community. The Cannon family's emphasis on education, civic duty, and social responsibility set a standard for future generations. Today, Wisteria Place still stands in Columbus, a tangible reminder of William R. Cannon Sr. and the early pioneers who helped build Mississippi.

The Meek Family Legacy - A Tale of Two Brothers

Following Cannon's death, the story of Wisteria Place became intertwined with the Meek family. William Cannon's daughter, Mary Louise, married Samuel Meek Jr., a prominent lawyer and statesman. Samuel had a much older brother named Alexander Meek, a man of many accomplishments.

Alexander was an Alabama attorney, a war hero of the Seminole Wars in Florida, a poet, editor of the Mobile Register, and even served as Speaker of the House for the Alabama legislature. His poem "The Red Eagle" about the Creek Indian chief William Weatherford gained him considerable literary acclaim in the South.

In a twist of fate, William Cannon's widow, Eliza, found love again with Alexander Meek. The couple married in September 1864, during the tumultuous final months of the Civil War. Alexander moved into Wisteria Place, bringing with him a vast library of legal and literary works that added to the home's intellectual atmosphere.

Unfortunately, their time together was brief, as Alexander passed away in November 1865 at the age of 51, possibly due to the stresses of the post-war period. His death left Eliza a widow for the second time in just seven years.

Eliza Cannon Meek continued to reside in Wisteria Place long after the deaths of both her husbands. She called the grand mansion home until her passing in 1901, at 84. During her long tenure, Eliza became known as a gracious hostess and a pillar of Columbus society. She maintained the house's reputation as a center of culture and refinement, hosting literary salons and musical evenings that were the talk of the town.

Curiously, while both William Cannon and Alexander Meek have marked graves in Friendship Cemetery, Eliza's final resting place remains a mystery. Legend suggests she lies between her two husbands, though no headstone bears her name. This peculiar absence has fueled speculation and ghost stories for generations, with some claiming to have seen Eliza's spirit wandering the cemetery grounds on moonlit nights.

Alexander Meek - Southern Statesman and Literary Figure

Alexander Beaufort Meek was born on July 17, 1814, in Columbia, South Carolina. His parents, Dr. Samuel Mills Meek and Ann McDowell Meek were of Scottish-Irish descent. When Alexander was five years old, his family moved to Tuscaloosa, Alabama, a decision that would profoundly shape his life and career.

Meek's early education was likely conducted at home and in local schools. As a young man, he pursued higher education first at the University of Georgia in Athens. However, he soon transferred to the newly established University of Alabama in Tuscaloosa, which had opened its doors in 1831. Meek was among the university's early students, graduating in 1833 with distinction. His time at the University of Alabama laid the foundation for his intellectual journey and instilled in him a lifelong love of learning.

After graduating, Meek wasted no time in pursuing a legal career in Nashville, Tennessee. He studied law under the tutelage of experienced attorneys, a common practice at the time. His dedication and natural aptitude for legal matters allowed him to progress quickly. In

1835, just two years after finishing his university studies, Meek was admitted to the Alabama bar. This rapid advancement showcased his intelligence, drive, and commitment to his chosen profession.

Meek's interests extended beyond law into the realm of politics and public service. In the mid-1830s, he became the editor of Tuscaloosa's democratic newspaper, *The Flag of the Union*. This position allowed him to engage with current events, shape public opinion, and hone his writing skills. As editor, Meek covered a wide range of topics, from local issues to national politics, providing insightful commentary that caught the attention of Alabama's political elite.

Demonstrating his commitment to his country, Meek volunteered in the U.S. Army during the Second Seminole War in Florida (1835-1842). He served as a lieutenant in the Alabama Volunteers, gaining firsthand experience in military affairs and national security. This service not only broadened his perspective but also enhanced his reputation as a man willing to serve his country in various capacities.

Meek's talents were quickly recognized by Alabama's political leadership. In 1836, at the remarkably young age of 23, he was appointed Attorney General of Alabama by Governor Clement Comer Clay. This appointment marked him as a rising star in the state's political scene and demonstrated the trust placed in his legal acumen and judgment despite his youth.

In the early 1840s, Meek served as a probate judge in Tuscaloosa County. This role gave him valuable experience in the judicial system, particularly in matters related to wills, estates, and guardianships. His fair-minded approach and thorough understanding of the law earned him respect from both colleagues and the public.

Meek's reputation extended beyond state borders, leading to an appointment in the federal treasury under President James K. Polk in 1845. In this role, he gained insight into national financial policies and expanded his network in Washington, D.C. Later, he worked as a federal attorney for the Southern District of Alabama, prosecuting cases on behalf of the United States government. These positions broadened his legal expertise and gave him a unique perspective on the relationship between state and federal governance.

In 1852-1853, Meek was elected to the Alabama legislature, representing Tuscaloosa County. During his time in the state house, he made significant contributions to Alabama's development. His most notable achievement was crafting and championing a law to establish Alabama's public school system. This legislation laid the groundwork for universal education in

the state, demonstrating Meek's commitment to social progress and his belief in the transformative power of education.

Meek served as the first President of the American Chess Congress. He was good friends with the parents of chess genius Paul Morphy. Meek played five public games against the brilliant yet eccentric 17-year-old Paul in Alabama in 1854. Meek lost each game but earned great respect among the chess community for the skill with which he challenged the tactically brilliant Morphy.

Meek's political career reached new heights when he served as Speaker of the Alabama House of Representatives in 1859. In this influential position, he guided the state's legislative agenda, mediated debates, and showcased his leadership skills. His tenure as Speaker was marked by efforts to modernize Alabama's infrastructure and economy while navigating the increasing tensions between North and South.

Alexander Meek was not only a skilled politician and lawyer but also a talented writer and orator. His literary works spanned various genres and reflected his deep interest in history, culture, and the human experience. Some of his most notable works include:

"The Red Eagle" (1855 – still in print): This narrative poem tells the story of William Weatherford, also known as Red Eagle, a Creek chief who played a significant role in the Creek War of 1813-1814. Meek's poem blends historical fact with romantic imagery, presenting a sympathetic portrayal of Weatherford and exploring themes of cultural conflict and personal honor.

Romantic Passages in Southwestern History (1856 - still in print): This collection of historical essays and sketches focuses on the early history of Alabama and neighboring states. Meek's work combines careful research with vivid storytelling, bringing to life the adventures of explorers, settlers, and Native Americans in the region.

Songs and Poems of the South (1856 - still in print): This volume showcases Meek's poetic talents and his deep connection to Southern culture. The collection includes lyrical pieces celebrating the natural beauty of the South, as well as more reflective works on themes of love, loss, and regional identity.

"Balaklava": Published under a pseudonym in October 1854, this poem about the Crimean War demonstrates Meek's interest in global events, and his ability to craft stirring verse caught the eye of Queen Victoria and peeved Sir Alfred Tennyson who responded in December 1854 with his poem "The Charge of the Light Brigade".

These works showcased Meek's creativity, his fascination with history, and his ability to capture the spirit of the American South in prose and verse. His writing often romanticized the region's past while also grappling with its complexities and contradictions.

Despite later misconceptions that sometimes portrayed him as a secessionist, Alexander Meek was strongly opposed to secession and a pro-Unionist who believed in the strength and promise of a united America. He was convinced that the South had a stronger position within the Union than outside of it; however, he was staunchly pro-slavery.

Meek argued that secession would be economically disastrous for the South and could lead to a devastating war. He believed that the South's interests could be better protected through political negotiation and compromise within the existing constitutional framework. In speeches and writings, he urged his fellow Southerners to resist the call for secession and to work towards reconciliation with the North.

These views set him apart from many of his contemporaries in the South and demonstrated his independent thinking. However, they also put him at odds with the growing secessionist movement in Alabama and throughout the region. As the secession crisis intensified in 1860-1861, Meek found himself increasingly isolated politically, though he continued to advocate for the preservation of the Union until the outbreak of the Civil War.

Alexander Meek married twice. His first wife was Emma Donaldson Slater of Mobile, whom he married in the early 1840s. After her death, he married Eliza Jane Cannon in 1864 in Columbus, Mississippi and moved into Wisteria Place. While records of his family life are limited, it's clear that Meek balanced his public career with his private responsibilities as a husband and stepfather to Eliza's children from a previous marriage.

Meek passed away on November 1, 1865, at the age of 51, in Columbus, Mississippi. His death came just months after the end of the Civil War, a conflict that had challenged many of his beliefs and hopes for the nation. He left behind a legacy as a talented orator, writer, and statesman who had played a significant role in shaping Alabama's political and cultural landscape during the antebellum period.

A contemporary, Reverend Philip Neely, offered a glowing description of Meek, calling him

Death of Judge A. B. Meek.

It falls to our sad lot to announce the death of A B. Meek—a man whose worth and intellect is too well known and appreciated throughout this Southern land, to need a word of ours to add lustre to his fame. He died yesterday morning, about 2 o'clock, in the bosom of his affectionate family. His funeral will take place this morning at ten o'clock, from his late residence.

In announcing the death of this eminent man—this kind hearted and genial gentleman—this scholar and poet—this orator and legislator and judge—this editor and embryo historian—we deplore our incompetency to put in words what we feel and wish to express.

We have enjoyed the pleasure and honor of an intimate personal acquaintance with him since 1840. He has ever proved to us—as he has to many—a warm hearted friend—one who sought not to detect faults and errors in those with whom he associated, but was always ready to throw the mantle of charity over their short comings.

He was modest and unassuming.—His hand was ever ready to help the struggling, who sought his advice or assistance. Courteous, affable and kind to all who come in contact with him, he has passed to his grave, honored, beloved, and deplored by all who knew him.

Abler pens than ours we trust, will do justice to his memory.—*Columbus Sentinel.*

The Daily Mississippian; 09 Nov 1865, Thu; Page 2

"beyond comparison the handsomest man of his time" and "one of the most remarkable men who ever lived in Mobile." This praise spoke not only to Meek's physical appearance but also to his intellectual gifts and personal charisma.

Alexander Beaufort Meek's life embodied the complexities and contradictions of the antebellum South. He was a man of letters and law, a political leader who rose quickly through the ranks of Alabama politics, and a staunch Unionist in a region moving inexorably towards secession. His contributions to Alabama's legal system, education policy, and literary culture left an indelible mark on the state's history.

Meek's career spanned a period of profound change in the United States, from the optimism of the Jacksonian era to the tragedy of the Civil War. Throughout these tumultuous times, he sought to serve his state and nation to the best of his abilities, often taking principled stands that put him at odds with prevailing political winds.

As a writer, Meek helped to articulate a distinctive Southern literary voice, one that celebrated the region's history and natural beauty while also grappling with its social and political challenges. His poems and historical works continue to offer valuable insights into the cultural life of the nineteenth-century South.

Despite some posthumous misconceptions about his political allegiances, Meek's true legacy is that of a thoughtful, talented individual who sought to bridge the growing divide between North and South. His life story serves as a reminder of the diverse political views that existed in the antebellum South and the personal costs often associated with going against the tide of popular opinion.

Today, Alexander Beaufort Meek is remembered as an important figure in Alabama's (and by extension Columbus') history, a man whose contributions to law, literature, and public service helped to shape the state during a critical period in its development. His story continues to offer valuable lessons about the role of the intellectual in public life and the challenges of maintaining one's principles in times of political upheaval.

Samuel M. Meek: A Southern Lawyer's Journey

Samuel M. Meek Jr. was born in 1835 in Tuscaloosa, Alabama, the son of Reverend Dr. Samuel Meek Sr. and Anna McDowell Meek. Destined for public service and legal prominence, he attended the University of Alabama, where Meek distinguished himself academically and as a student leader. The university during this period was a crucible of Southern intellectual thought, preparing young men like Meek for leadership roles in law, politics, and society. His rigorous legal studies focused on constitutional law, criminal jurisprudence, property rights, and civil procedure. After completing his education at the University of Alabama, Meek pursued a career in law, establishing himself as a formidable attorney in the Mississippi legal landscape.

He first arrived in September 1851 in modern day Lowndes County to interview as a school master with the Choctaw Agency at Bachelor's Retreat in Oktibbeha County. He began a school for young men in the area and began to visit with influential prairie families and Columbus residents. Col. William Barry, Dr. Lipscomb, and William Cannon took Meek under their wings and helped him grow his school as well as included him in local social gatherings. He did some "lawyering" in between. It was during this time he met his future wife Mary Louisa Cannon who had quite the crush on him. She described him as having "beautiful dark hair and dark eyes…" and that she "hope he will marry a lady worthy of him."

In 1856, Meek married Mary Louisa (Maynie) Cannon, daughter of Eliza and William Cannon. Their union produced at least 13 children, 11 of whom were named. Standing an impressive 6'3" tall, Meek cut an imposing figure both in the courtroom and in his community. Contemporary accounts describe him as articulate and commanding, physically robust, possessing a penetrating intellect, while maintaining a dignified demeanor. From 1856-1858 Samuel, an active Mason served as the grand master of the Grand Lodge of Mississippi.

During the Civil War, Meek served with distinction as a Lieutenant Colonel, fighting in both the 5th and 1st Mississippi Infantry regiments. This military experience would later inform his legal and political career.

Considered one of the finest criminal lawyers in the South, Meek was known for his legal acumen and professional demeanor. His reputation was further enhanced by his involvement in the Masonic order, a significant social and professional network of the time. Meek quickly rose to prominence as a criminal attorney, serving in several key legal positions. He served as a Lowndes County Prosecutor and then District Attorney for the 1st Judicial District of Mississippi. He also served in the state Senate for multiple terms.

An interesting chapter in Meek's life involves a sensationalized rumor about a duel with General Reuben Davis. The rumored confrontation with General Reuben Davis exemplifies the complex social dynamics of the era. While sensationalist newspapers initially suggested a dramatic confrontation, subsequent investigations revealed the story as manufactured gossip, highlighting the media's role in crafting narratives. However, the editor of The Clarion quickly debunked these claims as nothing more than sensationalist gossip.

Davis was alive and well and still representing criminals in courtrooms around the South. Meek continued to serve as a state senator, maintaining his reputation as a distinguished legal professional.

On December 21, 1901, Meek, age 66, passed away in Columbus, Mississippi. His family held the funeral at the First Methodist Church in downtown Columbus, and he laid him to rest in Friendship Cemetery.

Samuel M. Meek represents a quintessential Southern professional of the post-Civil War era - a veteran, lawyer, politician, and community leader who  navigated the complex social and professional landscapes of 19th-century Mississippi with skill and integrity. He advanced Mississippi's legal infrastructure and represented a generation bridging antebellum and modern legal practices. Meek's life offers a nuanced lens into the 19th-century Southern gentleman.

Wisteria Place Echoes of the Past

The early morning mist clung to the streets of Columbus, Mississippi like a ghostly veil. Sarah, a high school senior spending her summer volunteering at the local historical society, found herself on the porch of Temple Heights, an antebellum mansion overlooking Sixth Avenue. As she settled into a rocking chair with her book, the eerie stillness was broken by an unexpected sound.

Clip-clop, clip-clop.

Sarah's ears perked up. A horse? In downtown Columbus? Curiosity piqued, she set her book aside and leaned against one of the grand columns, straining to see through the thick fog.

The rhythmic hoofbeats grew louder, accompanied by the labored breathing of a horse climbing the gentle slope. A man's voice, rich with a soft Mississippi drawl, drifted through the air:

"Come on now, Jake. Almost home now..."

As Sarah watched, two figures emerged from the mist – a Black man leading a roan horse with a dark mane. Atop the horse, slumped over its neck, was another figure dressed in what appeared to be a Confederate uniform.

The trio turned up the driveway of Wisteria Place, a nearby house with a small yard and no visible stable. Sarah's breath caught in her throat as she realized something was amiss. The man leading the horse gently placed his hand on the back of the rider.

"We're home now," he said softly.

In an instant, as the morning sun began to burn away the fog, the men and horse simply vanished before Sarah's eyes.

Heart pounding, Sarah rushed inside to share her experience with Mrs. Hawkins, a history curator in town. As they pored over old records and family histories, a story began to emerge:

Captain Samuel Meek, son-in-law to the original owners of Wisteria Place, had served in the Confederate infantry. He had contracted malaria during the war, and legend told of a loyal enslaved man who had accompanied him and brought him home to recover.

"But Mrs. Hawkins," Sarah exclaimed, "Captain Meek died in 1901. How could I have seen...?"

The older woman smiled knowingly. "My dear, some memories are so powerful, they leave imprints on the very fabric of time. What you witnessed was an echo of the past, a moment frozen in history."

As Sarah returned to Temple Heights that day, her mind whirled with possibilities. The ghostly encounter had sparked a passion for local history she never knew she possessed. Little did she know, this was just the beginning of a summer filled with supernatural discoveries and a deepening connection to the rich, complex past of her hometown.

She couldn't wait to uncover what other secrets Wisteria Place – and the rest of Columbus – might be hiding.

(Note: This excerpt is from an future collection of stories about the ghosts and legends of Columbus by Patricia Shannon Evans.)

The Legacy of Wisteria Place

Wisteria Place stands today as a silent witness to the joys, sorrows, and mysteries of generations past. From William Cannon's brief residency to Eliza's long tenure, the house has absorbed the stories of those who called it home.

The mansion has weathered the storms of history - from the Civil War to the Great Depression - and emerged as a treasured landmark. Its rooms echo with the laughter of long-ago parties, the heated discussions of wartime strategy, and the quiet grief of widowhood.

As visitors walk its halls and explore its grounds, they can't help but feel the weight of history – and perhaps catch a glimpse of William Cannon's restless spirit, keeping watch over his beloved home. The creaking floorboards, the whisper of curtains in a seemingly still room, and the occasional unexplained footstep all add to the mystique of Wisteria Place.

Today, Wisteria Place serves as a museum and event venue, allowing new generations to connect with the rich tapestry of Southern history. Whether one believes in ghosts or not, there's no denying the palpable sense of the past that permeates every corner of this grand old house, inviting us to step back in time and imagine life in the antebellum South.

Wisteria Place – Robert Calcagno 2024

About The Author

Patricia Shannon Evans is a local author, podcaster, and public historian. She is a fifth/sixth generation Mississippian. Her deep Southern roots and extensive family are rich with great characters and champion storytellers.

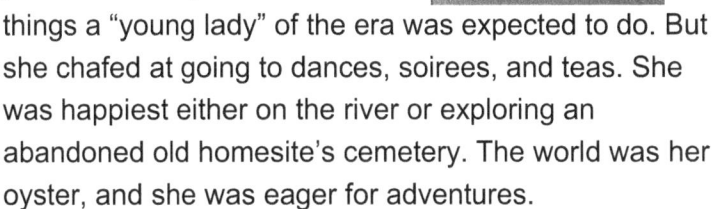

Evans attended Ole Miss, joined a sorority and did all the things a "young lady" of the era was expected to do. But she chafed at going to dances, soirees, and teas. She was happiest either on the river or exploring an abandoned old homesite's cemetery. The world was her oyster, and she was eager for adventures.

She left soon after college, first for the Middle East and then Europe. Her three children (Taylor, Jenny, and Colin) claim their childhood was spent either sweating in a tent in tick and snake infested woods or freezing in castles and fortresses on wind and rainswept moors.

Evans returned home in the middle of the Covid epidemic and earned an MFA in Creative Writing at Mississippi University for Women. She podcasts at *Tombigbee Tales* about local history old and new. She also posts a one-minute video on the Tombigbee Tales YouTube channel every day about people buried in Mississippi cemeteries (mostly Lowndes County).

Bibliography of Historical Sources

Primary Sources
1. Cannon, William R. *Biographical and Historical Memoirs of Mississippi*. Chicago: Goodspeed Publishing Company, 1891.

2. Meek, Samuel Mills. *Private Diary of S. M. Meek of Columbus, Miss., for October, November and December 1894*. Manuscript, 20 × 28 cm.

3. O'Neall, John Belton. *Biographical Sketches of the Bench and Bar of South Carolina*. Charleston, SC: S.G. Courtenay & Co., 1859.

Manuscript Collections
1. *Speeches of the Students of the I.O.O.F. Collegiate High School, July, 1854*. Manuscript, 21.5 × 36 cm.

2. Meek, Samuel Mills Jr. *Diary of Samuel Mills Meek, Jr. 1851-1854*. Transcription.

Miscellaneous Addresses

1. Meek, Samuel M. *Address before the Odd Fellows Collegiate High School*. N.d., 44 pp., 20 × 25 cm.

2. *Address to "Citizens and Soldiers"*. N.d., 51 pp., 19.5 × 24.5 cm.

Online Resources

1. "First American Chess Congress Opponents." Retrieved from http://www.edochess.ca/batgirl/congressplayers.html

2. "Southern Literary Messenger Archives." University of Pennsylvania Online Books Library. Retrieved November 7, 2018.